May you have Peace and l.♡ . . . .
in you life.
Narte Tayne
2013

Meet Naiche

To the memory of Roberta Blackgoat.
May future generations carry forth her love
and work for Mother Earth. —G.T.

Beyond Words Publishing, Inc.
20827 N.W. Cornell Road, Suite 500
Hillsboro, OR 97124-9808
503-531-8700
www.beyondword.com

Project Director and Head of Publications, NMAI: Terence Winch
Series Editor, NMAI: Amy Pickworth
Designer: Andrea L. Boven, Boven Design Studio, Inc.

For information about the National Museum of the American Indian, visit the NMAI website at www.AmericanIndian.si.edu.

Printed in Korea
Distributed to the book trade by Publisher's Group West

First edition
10 9 8 7 6 5 4 3 2 1

LIBRARY OF CONGRESS CATALOGING-IN-PUBLICATION DATA
Tayac, Gabrielle.
    Meet Naiche: a native boy from the Chesapeake Bay area / by Gabrielle Tayac; with
    photographs by John Harrington.—1st ed.
        p. cm. – (My world—Young Native Americans today)
    Summary: Details a day in the life of a rural Maryland boy of Piscataway and Apache descent, looking at his family, the history of his tribe, and some traditional ceremonies and customs that are still observed today.
    ISBN 1-58270-072-9
        1. Tayac, Naiche Woosah—Juvenile literature. 2. Piscataway Indians—Juvenile literature. 3. Piscataway Indians—Biography—Juvenile literature. 4. Apache Indians—Juvenile literature. [1. Tayac, Naiche Woosah. 2. Piscataway Indians. 3. Indians of North America—Maryland. 4. Apache Indians. 5. Indians of North America—New Mexico.] I. Title. II. Series.

E99.C873 T39 2002
975.2004'973—dc21   2002066651

The National Museum of the American Indian, Smithsonian Institution, is dedicated to working in collaboration with the indigenous peoples of the Americas to protect and foster Native cultures throughout the Western Hemisphere. The museum's publishing program seeks to augment awareness of Native American beliefs and lifeways, and to educate the public about the history and significance of Native cultures.

The museum's George Gustav Heye Center in Manhattan opened in 1994; its Cultural Resources Center opened in Suitland, Maryland, in 1998; and in 2004, the museum will open its primary facility on the National Mall in Washington, D.C.

Meet Naiche

A Native Boy from the Chesapeake Bay Area

Gabrielle Tayac

With photographs by John Harrington

My World: Young Native Americans Today

National Museum of the American Indian
Smithsonian Institution
in association with
Beyond Words Publishing, Inc.

Hi! My name is Gabrielle Tayac (pronounced TIE-ack). You can call me Gabi. My family comes from many different cultures. My mother is Jewish and my father is Native American. My husband is from Colombia, a country in South America. We have a six-year-old son, Sebastian, who is proud of all these cultures, and a new baby daughter, Jansikwe.

I work at the National Museum of the American Indian in Washington, D.C., where I teach visitors about the Native peoples of North, Central, and South America. There are hundreds of unique American Indian tribes, nations, and communities. Each one has its own language, identity, history, and spirituality.

My tribe is the Piscataway (pronounced pih-SKAT-away). For thousands of years, we have lived in Maryland and the Chesapeake Bay region. Soon you'll meet a very special person from my tribe—my cousin, Naiche (pronounced NAY-chee).

A lot of people think that all Native Americans live on reservations, or only in the western or southwestern United States. But this isn't true. I grew up in New York City. Many American Indians from many different tribes live there and in other big cities as well. Naiche lives with his mother and father in a rural area in Maryland. Maryland and the Chesapeake Bay region have a long Native American history—just like the whole American continent!

The Piscataway people are still alive today. Hundreds of years ago, our villages were built along the Potomac River—in fact, the word *piscataway* means "where the waters blend." We lived in longhouses, called *witchotts* (pronounced WHICH-otts), made from wood and bark. Today we live in houses and apartments just like you. The women grew corn, beans, squash, sunflowers, and tobacco, while the men hunted in the forests. Everyone caught fish, crabs, and oysters. Although Piscataway grown-ups today have jobs just like your parents, fishing, gardening, and hunting are activities that some of our people still enjoy. The Piscataway used to travel by canoe and on foot over many trails. Now our people still have fun canoeing and hiking, but we mostly travel by car, train, bus, and airplane—just like you!

The Piscataway language belongs to the Algonquian (pronounced al-GONK-ee-yun) cultural family. The Algonquian peoples live in areas ranging from northern Canada to the southern United States. Nobody really speaks Piscataway anymore, and that makes us sad. But many American Indians still speak their native languages and are bilingual in English.

OPPOSITE: This watercolor is by English artist John White. He traveled to North America in 1585, and his illustrations of what he saw there give us some of the most important records of the Native peoples of the Chesapeake Bay area from that time. This painting shows two men fishing with spears, while others, in a dugout canoe, use nets attached to long poles.
(COURTESY OF THE BRITISH MUSEUM)

The manner of their fishing.

A Cannow.

Kids can be teachers, too. In one traditional story, a brother and sister teach grown-ups about forgiveness. The brother and sister fight, and the sister storms away. Later, he feels bad about their argument and wants to talk to her, but she will have none of it. Every time he tries to speak to her, she walks away. He feels truly sorry, so the Creator takes pity on him and tries to help him. The Creator places a pile of ripe blackberries in the sister's path, hoping to catch her attention. The sister sees the blackberries but passes right by them. Then the Creator places a pile of ripe raspberries in her path, but again, she walks right by. Then the Creator places a pile of ripe strawberries in her path. Ahhh! This catches her attention. The sister stops to eat the luscious berries and ends up sharing them with her brother. And as they eat, they forget what they were arguing about in the first place.

This story reminds us that just a little sweetness helps us to overcome bitterness and forgive each other.

OPPOSITE: These photographs from about 1911 show Nanticoke (pronounced NAN-tee-coke) kids playing a game called "Bear in Ring." It looks like fun! (NMAI P1304 AND 1305; PHOTOS BY FRANK G. SPECK)
BELOW: This map shows the locations of many of the Native communities of the Chesapeake Bay area. The Piscataway and Nanticoke tribes are neighbors. Both tribes are Algonquian, and are descended from the Lenape (pronounced len-AH-pay), or Delaware, Indians. (REPRINTED FROM THE HANDBOOK OF NORTH AMERICAN INDIANS, COURTESY OF THE SMITHSONIAN NATIONAL MUSEUM OF NATURAL HISTORY)

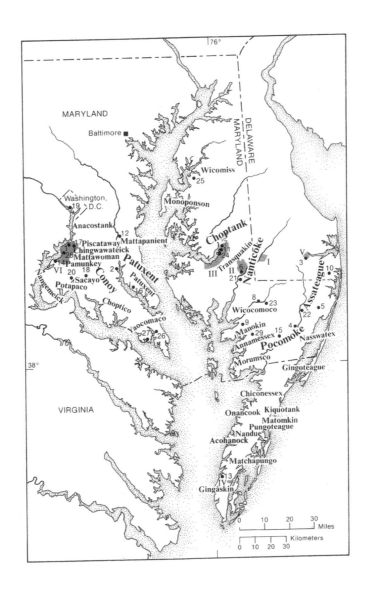

hildren are very important people in Native culture. Now, let's go spend time with Naiche and see what he has to teach us about the Piscataway.

Hi, I'm Naiche, and I'm an American Indian. My life is probably a lot like yours. I have a dog, a bike that I love to ride, and my own room, which is sometimes very messy! I live with my mom and dad and go to public school. I have a lot of friends. Some are Native, some are not.

This is my room. It's pretty clean today. Our house is in the country and sometimes I can see hawks or eagles from my window. It's early springtime outside. This is an important week for my family and me. This is when we honor the awakening of Mother Earth after a long winter. It is our time to give thanks for new life and for young people—like us! Around this time of year, people all over the world are celebrating Earth Day. My people have celebrated the Earth for thousands of years.

My mom is San Carlos Apache (pronounced uh-PATCH-ee). She grew up in Arizona on the San Carlos reservation. The Piscataway language is pretty much gone now, but my mom can speak Apache as well as she speaks English. She came to the East Coast because she was in the Army and worked at the Pentagon. Then she met my dad and decided to stay. Native American veterans have an important place in our culture. They continue the tradition of brave warriors who take care of their people.

My dad is Piscataway. He and my grandfather own a furniture store together, but Dad also spends a lot of time making traditional crafts, such as featherwork. His projects are spread all over our house.

OPPOSITE TOP: Naiche's dad is a talented featherworker. He makes a lot of their family's traditional clothing. Here, he is working on a feather bustle that Naiche will wear at powwows this summer. Hanging on the wall behind them is a bustle that belongs to Naiche's brother, Phillip. You can see a picture of Phillip wearing his bustle on page 18.
OPPOSITE BOTTOM: Naiche's mom, Joyce, showing him some of her military awards.

My full name is Naiche Woosah Tayac, and I guess that says a lot about me. I was named in honor of a great Chiricahua (pronounced cheer-eh-COW-wah) Apache leader, Naiche. He was born into the Chokonen band of Apaches and lived from about 1856 to 1921. Naiche was a good friend of the famous warrior Geronimo, whose Apache name was Goyathlay (pronounced goy-ANHK-lah). Together Goyathlay and Naiche stood up for Native American rights.

Woosah (pronounced woo-SAH) was my great-great-grandfather's name. Tayac, in the Piscataway language, means "head chief," a traditional title that my family holds in our tribe.

ABOVE: Naiche (left), after whom Naiche Tayac was named, and his friend Goyathlay, also known as Geronimo, in a photo taken around 1884. (NMAI P6727)

Last summer I went to Arizona to visit my mom's family on the San Carlos Apache Indian Reservation. The Apache call themselves *n'nee* (pronounced nah-NAY), which means "the people." Native Americans used to live freely all over North and South America. A lot of Native peoples don't think that Columbus discovered America, because their ancestors were already here. When European settlers began arriving in America, many American Indians were killed or forced to move to new places, sometimes far away. I don't think that was fair at all. Indian people couldn't understand why they had to leave their homelands.

In 1875, the Apaches were ordered to move to a reservation at San Carlos, in southeast Arizona. The reservation land was set aside by the U.S. government for the Native Americans. Life on the reservation was terribly hard when they got there. Many people died from sickness and hunger. Some Apaches, including Naiche and Goyathlay, wanted to stay free. They fought against the government for several years before they were forced to surrender and were put into prison. Goyathlay and Naiche are heroes for many American Indians today.

My mom grew up on the same San Carlos reservation. Thousands of Apaches still live there. There were problems when reservations started, and there are still some problems today, but reservations are also places where our cultures are alive and where we share our love of family and home. During our visit, Mom was busy helping her family protest the building of a giant telescope on Mt. Graham, a place that is sacred to the Apache people. I had a lot of fun running around with my cousins and eating tortillas!

The National Museum of the American Indian has many objects—more than 800,000!—in its collection. The objects shown here were all made by Apache people.

TOP: San Carlos Apache beaded hide shirt, ca. 1880. Arizona. (NMAI 20.2049)
BOTTOM: Apache deerhide playing cards, ca. 1880. (NMAI 9455)
OPPOSITE TOP: San Carlos Apache doll, early 20th century. Arizona. (NMAI 8.5592)

My dad is also involved in protecting our people's traditions. He gives presentations at schools and organizations to help people understand what Native American culture is about. Another way people can learn something about American Indians is by coming to our powwows. Powwows are American Indian gatherings where we sing, dance, hold contests, and sell crafts.

Powwows usually take place in the spring and summer, and I get really excited during this time of year. At powwows I get to see a lot of my friends who don't go to my school, and we have fun celebrating. My brother Phillip is a very good dancer, and I am learning. At powwows, we also get to eat lots of delicious food, like frybread and buffalo burgers.

RIGHT: This is Naiche's brother Phillip performing a dance. He lives in California, but they get to see each other on holidays.
OPPOSITE: Sometimes Naiche joins his dad when he does school presentations.
(BOTH COURTESY OF THE TAYAC FAMILY)

When I see Native Americans used as team mascots or in ads, I feel angry. It's like my own family is being used or made fun of. There are more than 500 American Indian tribes in the U.S., and we are all very different. We don't run around with tomahawks. We don't all ride horses. We don't usually wear moccasins or feathers to school. But sometimes we dance special dances and sing special songs. These songs and dances teach us about who we are and about the world around us. These things are important in our cultures.

Many people don't understand why some Native Americans, like me, wear their hair long or look different from others. For us, having long hair means that we are proud of our ancestors.

*M*y grandfather is the chief of the Piscataway Nation. He is our spiritual and political leader, and his name is Billy Tayac, but I call him Pop.

Long before the White House was built, the Piscataway spent a lot of time on the land that is now Washington, D.C., hunting, trading, and fishing. Today, many Piscataway people live and work in Washington—just like my cousin Gabi.

While many of our people live in Maryland, others live all over the United States and in different countries.

OPPOSITE: Here are Naiche's grandfather and father in 1999 at the groundbreaking for the National Museum of the American Indian in Washington. Chief Tayac is offering tobacco to bless the site where the museum will be built. He and Naiche's father also sang at the ceremony. Hundreds of Native people from all over North and South America came to the National Mall to celebrate that day. Sitting on the stage behind Chief Tayac and Naiche's father are (from left) Senator Ben Nighthorse Campbell (Northern Cheyenne) of Colorado (partially obscured by feather fan), Senator Daniel Inouye of Hawai'i, NMAI director W. Richard West, and now-former Smithsonian Secretaries I. Michael Heyman and Robert McCormick Adams. (©1999 SMITHSONIAN INSTITUTION)

$\mathcal{B}$efore I catch the school bus I eat breakfast with my mom and dad. I especially like to eat chipped beef and gravy, but we usually only get to eat that on the weekends when we cook big family brunches. Then I get on the bus and ride to school with my friends.

I always look forward to gym class—that's my favorite. In science, we're learning about plants and photosynthesis, and in math we're doing fractions. I also like going to the computer lab. I play many different sports, but soccer is my favorite because a lot of my friends are on my team.

After school my mom picks me up. Sometimes I ride the bus, but this is Friday, and the beginning of a special weekend.

Naiche's day at school probably looks a lot like yours.

*T*onight is a big night. It is the start of the Awakening of Mother Earth celebration. My family and other people from my tribe are going down to the Moyaone (pronounced moy-OWN) burial grounds for a ceremony. Many generations of my ancestors are buried there. Archeologists say that my ancestors have lived at Moyaone for about 11,000 years, but the Piscataway believe that we have been here forever. Moyaone is very special to us.

During the ceremony we burn tobacco. That is the way we pray.

As it gets dark, we see some deer. We hear geese flying overhead—they are coming back for the spring. The Piscataway word for geese is *cohonk*. Say *cohonk, cohonk* really loud a few times and you will sound just like a goose! Mother Earth is starting to wake up.

When night comes, we build a fire to heat rocks for a purification ceremony in the sweatlodge. The sweatlodge is a little hut made out of willow branches. Rocks are heated in a fire and then brought inside the lodge, where water is poured over them to make steam. Dad tells everyone how the rocks are the oldest beings on the earth—he calls them "grandfathers." Pop says that the steam coming off them is the breath of the Creator.

The adults and some of the kids go into the sweatlodge to give thanks and to pray. Sometimes I help with the fire and bring the hot rocks to the sweatlodge on a pitchfork. It's hard work, but I do it with good feelings, knowing that my family and friends will be happy.

Tomorrow is the ceremony for the Awakening of Mother Earth.

The fire for heating the rocks is prepared in the pit in front of the sweatlodge.

At Moyaone there is a cedar tree planted where my great-grandfather is buried. The cedar is an important tree for the Piscataway people. Pop says that it is the tree of life. Cedar trees are especially sacred to us because we believe that the spirits of chiefs who lived long ago are part of that tree. Cedars are green all year round and their hearts are red, just like human hearts.

My great-grandfather, Pop's dad, was named Turkey Tayac. Many traditional American Indian names honor wild animals. The Piscataway believe that the wild turkey is a sacred bird. Grandpa Turkey was an important chief because he kept our history and ceremonies alive through times when there was a lot of racism against Native Americans.

Grandpa Turkey is buried under the cedar tree, so he is a part of a living thing. People often come to his tree at Moyaone to honor Chief Turkey and to remember other friends and family who have died. People leave gifts to show their love and respect.

ABOVE: Tobacco and a pipe tied to the cedar tree. (COURTESY OF THE TAYAC FAMILY)
MIDDLE: Tobacco ties on the cedar tree honor people who have died.
BOTTOM & OPPOSITE: Turkey Tayac was buried at Moyaone in the traditional Piscataway way in 1979. Moyaone is a national park and is controlled by the government, so Chief Turkey's relatives had to ask Congress for permission to bury his body there, even though this is where Piscataway chiefs have been buried for thousands of years. A plaque for Chief Tayac is beside the cedar tree that grows over his grave. (DETAIL COURTESY OF THE TAYAC FAMILY)

I wish Moyaone was not taken from my people. After the British came here, our land was taken over by settlers. Even land that had been made into a reservation for our ancestors was taken away during colonial times. Many of our people died from diseases and could no longer travel freely to hunt. The people who did survive had to move into swamps and other isolated places in the forest.

Many Piscataway left Maryland to live with other tribes like the Nanticoke, Lenape, and Iroquois (pronounced EAR-uh-coy) in the north. Even then, they were still forced to move from place to place as settlers continued to take their lands. Even though people fought very hard to keep their land, some were

moved as far away as Oklahoma and Canada. Times were hard for many years. The Piscataway who stayed in Maryland did farm work for the white settlers in the land that used to be our home. Some of our people earned enough money to buy their own land and farms.

Today our tribe is allowed to use Moyaone for ceremonies, but when we drive onto the property we have to be escorted by national park rangers. It seems strange that my people are restricted on the land that we have lived on for thousands of years. But I'm glad we can at least still go to Moyaone. Many places that are sacred to other American Indian tribes are not always as well protected or can't be used at all anymore.

ABOVE: The entrance to Piscataway National Park.

In 1608, Captain John Smith, the leader of the British colony Jamestown (and the man who, according to legend, was rescued by Pocahontas), sailed up the Potomac River to Moyaone, the center of the Piscataway chiefdom. The Piscataway were the leading tribe of an alliance of other related tribes including the Mattawoman (pronounced matt-uh-WOE-man), Nanjemoy (pronounced NAN-je-moy), Anacostan (pronounced anna-COST-un), and Portobacco (pronounced poor-toe-BACK-oh) peoples. At the time, Moyaone was a large stockaded town where close to 3,000 Piscataway people lived.

The town of Pomeiock and true forme of their houses, couered and inclosed some w matts, and some w barcks of trees. All compassed about w smale poles stock thick together in stedd of a wall.

The tribe had many kinds of chiefs for different purposes. The head chief was called a *tayac*. The tayac had to work just as hard as everyone else, and he did not get to make decisions alone. Holy people and a council, called the *matchcomoco* (pronounced match-KO-muh-ko), advised him. During times of peace, chiefs called *wisoes* (pronounced WEE-soes) helped the tayac. But when there was war, chiefs called *cockarouses* (pronounced COCK-uh-roo-sez) took over. Each town that was politically linked to Moyaone also had a chief called a *werowance* (pronounced where-oh-WAHNCE), or *weroansqua* (pronounced where-oh-WAHNCE-kwah) if the leader was a woman. By 1634, however, Moyaone was abandoned because of wars with the British and between the different tribes.

TOP: This John White painting from 1585 shows the stockaded village of Pomeiooc. Moyaone probably looked a lot like this.
BOTTOM: Another painting by John White, of a werowance, or chief.
(BOTH COURTESY OF THE BRITISH MUSEUM)

The morning after we visit Moyaone, I ride over to see my grandparents, Nana and Pop. My grandparents and my Aunt Nora's family live very close to me. My home includes more than just my house—"home" means all of my family and the land we live on together, which we call Tayac Territory. For Native Americans, family is very important. "Family" means more than just parents and kids—it means aunts, uncles, cousins, and grandparents, too. Some family groups are known as *clans*. A clan is a group of people within the tribe who believe they are descended from a particular animal. I am proud to be in the Beaver Clan, since beavers are the best builders and take good care of their families.

Nana isn't Indian, but she is very proud of our culture. We have a lot to do to get ready for today's Awakening of Mother Earth celebration. Nana is cooking and people are visiting. We will use tobacco and cedar in the ceremony, so I help Pop get them ready, crumbling tobacco and pulling cedar leaves off branches.

When the cedar leaves are burned, they bring in good spirits to help us think positively. When the tobacco leaves are burned, they send our prayers to the Creator. Tobacco is sacred in many American Indian cultures. I think it should not be abused by cigarette smoking.

A long time ago, Piscataway families lived in longhouses. Each clan had its own longhouse. A clan is a group of people who are related to each other from the distant past. Even if they are not related by blood, clan members still consider each other family. This is a way to keep people together and encourage them to help each other.

Naiche's grandmother, Shirley, is a good cook. She is busy making food while Naiche and his grandfather crumble up big leaves of dried tobacco. Tobacco is used in many different ceremonies, including the Awakening of Mother Earth ceremony.

e have so much to bring! Pop keeps our ceremonial items safe throughout the rest of the year and gets them out for this ceremony. Dad gets his drum ready. He and our friends will play drums and sing at the social tonight. Mom packs up our crafts, which she'll put out for sale later.

Everyone is rushing around, gathering things up and getting their folding chairs and blankets. Don't forget the tobacco and cedar! And don't forget to lock the food up in the van. One year the dogs got into the food and ate every bite of the dinner that was cooked for the social! Boy, was Nana steamed!

LEFT: Naiche and his dad carry a ceremonial drum to their van. Drumming and singing are important parts of the Awakening of Mother Earth ceremony and many other Native American events.
OPPOSITE: Special medicine bags are sometimes used to carry tobacco and pipes for ceremonies. This Lenape (Delaware) bag is from the collection of the National Museum of the American Indian. (NMAI 13.5886)

At Moyaone, we all come together. Some people come from far away to be here for this ceremony. It is a Piscataway ceremony, but people from different Native American nations attend, too. It is important for us to have our friends from all different cultures be here with us. Pop explains how the four colors that we use—black, yellow, red, and white—are also the four colors of people, and he talks about how we should all work together.

Our celebration is full of important symbols. The sacred red cedar tree carries the spirit of my great-grandfather. The spirit posts, which mark the four directions, protect the cedar tree and the people who are buried under it. The fire sends our prayers to the ancestors and to the Creator. Part of celebrating the Awakening of Mother Earth is celebrating springtime and new life, and sometimes there are special naming ceremonies for babies.

TOP: A fire is built in the middle of the circle.
RIGHT: Naiche's grandfather walks around the circle and blesses everyone there by touching each one's head with a feather.
OPPOSITE: Everyone gathers at Moyaone. It is a beautiful day.

$\mathcal{T}$he ceremony participants say their thanks for the renewal of Mother Earth. She has followed her original instructions, to wake up. Now we have followed our original instructions, to take care of her.

ABOVE : Naiche helps by passing out tobacco.
OPPOSITE : This is Roberta Blackgoat. She was an important Navajo elder from Arizona who worked to preserve her people's way of life at Big Mountain. She came a long way to join the ceremony, and she died as this book was being completed. It is dedicated to her memory.

The people attending the ceremony are purified through smoke made from burning cedar. In these pictures, Naiche "cedars" some other kids and his parents.

Singing and drumming are an important part of the ceremony.

After the ceremony, the grown-ups sit in the sunshine and visit while the kids play lacrosse. Later, everyone packs up and drives to a nearby building where we have the social. The kids play more games before we come indoors to eat dinner. Some of the adults and kids drum and sing, and people hang around all evening and talk.

Ceremonies like the Awakening of Mother Earth are also kind of like family reunions. Friends and family we don't get to see very often come to visit from far away.

TOP: After dinner, there's more drumming and singing.

RIGHT: People often sell handmade jewelry and other crafts at the social dinner. Naiche's mom is selling this jewelry.

OPPOSITE: Lacrosse is a very old American Indian sport. It's kind of like soccer, but instead of kicking the ball you pass it using a special stick with a net on the end.

*T*he day after the ceremony, my family and I go down to the Huckleberry for a walk. The Huckleberry is an area located along the cliffs of the Potomac and is part of the land that once belonged to my family. Sometimes I find fossilized shark teeth washed up on the shore here. Pretty cool! The Huckleberry is where my great-grandfather, Turkey Tayac, was born. He lived here with his mother, Janjan, and his father, Woosah. Woosah is my middle name.

At the Huckleberry, there are oyster heaps left over from hundreds of years ago. Native Americans caught oysters and roasted them. Roasting oysters preserves them so that they can last a long time, which was very important before people had refrigerators. Here, Naiche and his dad are checking out some oyster shells.

Near the Huckleberry is Port Tobacco, Maryland. Port Tobacco used to be a Piscataway town with a woman chief, called a weroansqua. But in 1641, the St. Ignatius Catholic Church was founded here and Catholic missionaries began converting the Piscataways to Christianity. Inside this church, built in 1798, are stained-glass windows showing the conversion of a tayac named Kittamaquund. Some Piscataways still worship here today.

Even though the missionaries wanted the Piscataway to give up their ceremonies, some kept practicing them. Often they held their ceremonies in secret. Other times they changed a ceremony so that the priests couldn't tell it was really a Native American tradition. For example, the Piscataway's Green Corn ceremony was disguised as the Catholic Feast of the Assumption picnic. In this way, the Piscataway were able to hold on to their beliefs and traditions after the coming of the Europeans and their religions. Today, many Native people practice Christianity.

Naiche likes climbing up the Huckleberry's cliffs and looking for feathers. He especially wants to find a wild turkey feather, because the wild turkey is a sacred bird and a symbol of the Piscataway.

A long time ago, Piscataway boys were taken away from their villages by the wise men of the communities so they could be taught important lessons about the values of being honorable men. This ceremony was known as the *huskanaw* (pronounced HUSS-can-aw). The Huckleberry is where my great-grandfather took my dad when it was his time to become a man. They spent several days here, then Chief Turkey gave my dad his name, Wild Turkey. When I'm old enough, the men in my family will bring me here to teach me what it means to be a Piscataway man.

But I like being a kid, and I'm not quite ready to grow up yet. And now it's time to go home. It's almost time for dinner, and we don't want to keep Nana waiting.

OPPOSITE: Naiche and his dad look out across the Potomac River.

A Piscataway Year

Calendars help us keep track of time. The calendar that is most widely used depends on numbered days and months. Today, Piscataway people use the same calendar most other people do, but they also know that there is a different way to understand time—a way that is not just counted by numbers.

The Piscataway traditionally lived according to the natural cycles of Mother Earth. Living "traditionally" means that people value the teachings of their ancestors. Each season of the year— summer, fall, winter, and spring—is still honored with ceremonies to give thanks for the gifts it brings.

The Piscataway see that all parts of the universe move in an unending circle. For example, a seed grows into a tree. The tree makes more seeds that grow into more trees. So, even if the tree dies, there is a part of it that is still being born over and over again. We believe that people should help to keep the natural circle from being broken. Remembering the ways of our ancestors at the four main points of the year is an important part of being a traditional Piscataway, even in the modern world.

Let's take a quick journey through the Piscataway year together.

SUMMER: THE GREEN CORN CEREMONY

The Piscataway and many other tribes in the eastern United States begin the ceremonial year in the late summer. In August, when all life has blossomed to its fullest, the corn has green husks and stalks and tastes fresh and sweet. This time is called the Green Corn. Other crops are also tender and ready for harvesting. It is a happy point of the year, when people can come together and celebrate Mother Earth's bounty.

Corn was the main food source for the Piscataway before Europeans settled Maryland. Corn is still enjoyed by the Piscataway and is considered to be one of the greatest gifts that Native Americans have given to the world.

The Green Corn ceremony, like all Piscataway ceremonies, takes place over four days at the Moyaone burial grounds. Piscataway people and their friends meet at Moyaone to give thanks for the corn and other crops. The Green Corn is also a time when women and children are the subjects of special prayers. The Piscataway believe that corn is female and the kernels are her children. Like a woman who has many babies, corn is a great life-giver.

FALL: THE FEAST OF
THE DEAD

In the autumn, Mother Earth starts to fall asleep. Where the Piscataway live, geese and other birds fly away for the winter, the leaves turn color and fall off of the trees, and the weather gets colder. This is a time when nature looks like it's dying, but we know that it's just changing, and that the plants and animals will come back in a few months.

This is the season when the Piscataway turn our attention to the memories of our ancestors. We take special care to remember all of the people we loved who have died. It is not a time to be sad, but a time to remember good things about the people who have died, and the happy, special moments that we shared with them before they went to the Spirit World.

In November, the Piscataway have a ceremony at Moyaone called the Feast of the Dead. A tobacco tie—a small bundle of cloth filled with tobacco—is made for each person who should be remembered. Everyone's tobacco ties are carried together in a procession to a sacred cedar tree, and people at the ceremony get up in front of others to talk about their loved ones. In this way the Feast of the Dead is really a celebration of many lives.

WINTER: THE MID-WINTER FESTIVAL

Winter can sometimes seem like a long and lonely time. Days are short and cold, and the world looks brown and dull. Mother Earth has been sleeping for a long time, and is not going to look different for a while longer. This is a time when the Piscataway see that it's important for people to gather together and cheer each other up.

A long time ago, the Piscataway used to leave their villages in the winter. Small family groups would travel together and go hunting for several months. Surviving the cold winters was not easy. At a certain point in the middle of the winter, all of the small groups would come back together for a short time to see who needed help and to spend time with other family and friends again.

Every February, the Piscataway have the Mid-Winter Festival to commemorate this time of our ancestors. There is not a large gathering at Moyaone, but people visit there to say prayers for the sleeping Mother Earth and for their relatives. A big indoor dinner is held on the weekend. It is lots of fun to talk, dance, and sing with family and friends at the festival, and it makes spring seem not so far away.

SPRING:
AWAKENING OF MOTHER EARTH CEREMONY

As you have read in this book, we celebrate renewal and new life at the Awakening of Mother Earth ceremony. We thank Mother Earth for waking up and acknowledge our responsibility to take care of her.